Contents

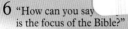

Special pull-out chart
Scriptures to help seekers after

4

"Isn't the Bible just a disconnected collection of ideas?"

WHAT'S THE PROBLEM?

"Reading the Bible is like traveling on a road that leads nowhere. There are so many different types of writing that just don't seem to link up with each other."

VARIETY

The books
• The Bible is not just one book. It is 66 books.

AUTHORS

Writers of the Bible include
• 40 different authors
• Non-Jews as well as Jews
• A farmer (Amos) as well as kings (Solomon and David)
• Fishermen (Peter, John) as well as a doctor (Luke)
• Philosophers (Writer of Ecclesiastes) as well as prophets (Isaiah and Jeremiah)

TYPES OF LITERATURE IN THE BIBLE

• History
• Prophecy
• Poetry
• A love story
• Parable
• Allegory
• Letters
• Gospels
• Apocalypse

LANGUAGES

The Bible was written in three languages:
• The Old Testament was written in Hebrew, with some Aramaic.
• The New Testament was written in Greek.

UNITY

Its theme
• Humankind turned against their Creator God. God in his love sent Jesus to bring humankind back to God.

ITS HARMONY

God is seen throughout the Bible as
• Creator
• Redeemer
• Judge

ITS PORTRAIT OF JESUS

• God and man
• The Bible books agree that Jesus was both fully human, the Son of Man and fully God, the Son of God.

WHAT'S THE CONCLUSION?

No other comparable literature in the world has such a harmony of outlook as provided by the writers of the Bible.

A QUOTE TO CHEW OVER

"All Scripture is God-breathed and is useful for teaching, rebuking, correcting and training in righteousness."
2 Timothy 3:16

"How can you say that Jesus is the focus of the Bible?"

WHAT'S THE PROBLEM?
"How can you say that Jesus is the focus of the Scriptures? Most of the Bible is taken up with the Old Testament before Jesus was even born."

JESUS WAS OUTSIDE HUMAN TIME
1. Jesus existed before time
It's no easy concept for our finite minds to comprehend this fact, but the Bible teaches that Jesus existed "in the beginning".

> "In the beginning was the Word, and the Word was with God, and the Word was God." *John 1:1*

"The Word was with God", so the Word is distinct from the Father. This phrase is saying, "Jesus was with God". The "Word was God", so Jesus was God in the fullest sense. This phrase is saying: "Jesus was God."

2. Jesus existed before Abraham
Jesus existed before Abraham, but not in human form.

> "'I tell you the truth,' Jesus answered, 'before Abraham was born, I am!'" *John 8:58*

THE FOCUS OF THE BIBLE
Amazing as it may seem, people manage to read the Bible and miss its main theme. The focus of the whole Bible is on God the Father and Jesus Christ. Jesus once told the Jews, "The Scriptures … testify about me." *John 5:39*

WHERE TO FIND JESUS IN THE BIBLE

1. Christ is in the law

The first five books of the Bible, the Pentateuch, were known as the books of the law in Jesus' day. Moses made the following prediction which was fulfilled literally by Jesus:

> "The Lord your God will raise up for you a prophet like me from among your own brothers. You must listen to him. … The Lord said to me … 'I will put my words in his mouth, and he will tell them everything I command him.'" *Deuteronomy 18:15,18*

The first chapter of Mark's Gospel is about Jesus' public ministry. The Greek word for "fulfilled" *peplerotai*, is a crucial one and comes in verse 15. "The time has come." *Mark 1:15*

2. Christ is in the prophets

Jesus fulfills the prophets' desire for peace and justice. "For to us a child is born, to us a son is given, and the government will be on his shoulders. And he will be called Wonderful Counsellor, Mighty God, Everlasting Father, Prince of Peace." *Isaiah 9:6*

3. Christ is in the writings

The third division of the Old Testament scriptures were known as "the writings" (the Psalms and the wisdom books). At Jesus' baptism and transfiguration the words used of him came from Psalm 2:7, "you are my Son" (see Matthew 3:17; Mark 9:7). As Martin Luther said, "The whole of Scripture deals with Christ throughout."

4. Christ is in the New Testament

The Gospels, letters of the New Testament and the Book of Revelation all center on Jesus Christ. At the end of his Gospel John says that he wrote so that his readers might have faith in Jesus. "Jesus did many other miraculous signs in the presence of his disciples, which are not recorded in this book. But these are written that you may believe that Jesus is the Christ, the Son of God, and that by believing you may have life in his name." *John 20:30-31*

WHAT'S THE CONCLUSION?

"Ignorance of the Scriptures is ignorance of Christ." *Jerome*

A QUOTE TO CHEW OVER

"The Bible is the portrait of Jesus Christ." *John Stott*

"How can the Bible be divinely inspired since it was written by human authors?"

WHAT'S THE PROBLEM?
"The Bible was written by fallible human authors. You may think it has some so-called inspired passages, but to say that the whole book is inspired by God is beyond reasonable belief."

Mechanical inspiration
Some Christians have given the impression that they believe that the Bible was downloaded in one zip-file from a heavenly site on the Internet. That is, the human authors of the Bible had no part in it.

But the Bible did not come into being in this way. God did not treat the authors of the Bible like dictating machines. Their styles and vocabulary remained their own. Their personalities were not ridden over roughshod. God used their backgrounds and experience to communicate a message that was distinctive to them. They wrote about what they knew and about what was burning in their hearts.

AUTHORS AND THEIR WRITINGS
So it should not surprise us that:

Writer	Topic
Amos, the small-time farmer, should write about	God's justice
Hosea, with a broken marriage, should write about	God's love
Isaiah, the noble courtier, should write about	God's kingly sovereignty
Paul, the fanatical Pharisee, should write about	grace and faith
James, the good man, should write about	good deeds
John, the beloved disciple, should write about	love
Peter, in the middle of persecution, should write about	hope

Human research not incompatible with divine inspiration

Sometimes the authors of the Bible received God's message through visions, or dreams, or from angels. At such times they may have been hardly conscious about what was going on.

At other times they took painstaking trouble to ensure that everything they wrote down was accurate.

Dr Luke, the author of Luke's Gospel, has been shown to be a reliable historian. Careful investigation was his hallmark.

> "Many have undertaken to draw up an account of the things that have been fulfilled among us, just as they were handed down to us by those who from the first were eye-witnesses and servants of the word. Therefore, since I myself have carefully investigated everything from the beginning, it seemed good also to me to write an orderly account for you, most excellent Theophilus, so that you may know the certainty of the things you have been taught." *Luke 1:1-4*

Dual authorship

Scripture is both the word of God and the word of men.

> "God spoke ... through the prophets." *Hebrews 1:1*

> "For prophecy never had its origin in the will of man, but men spoke from God as they were carried along by the Holy Spirit." *2 Peter 1:21*

In the same sentence, Luke calls the law "the Law of Moses" and "the Law of the Lord." *Luke 2:22-23*

A QUOTE TO CHEW OVER

> "The dual authorship of Scripture is an important truth to be carefully guarded. On the one hand, God spoke, revealing the truth and preserving the human authors from error, yet without violating their personality. On the other hand, men spoke, using their own faculties freely, yet without distorting the divine message.
>
> "Their words were truly their own words. But they were (and still are) also God's words, so that what Scripture says, God says."
>
> *John Stott, Understanding the Bible, Scripture Union, 1972, p. 185.*

"Is there any evidence to support the vast claims the Bible makes?"

WHAT'S THE PROBLEM?
"The Bible claims to be inspired by God.
> 'All Scripture is God-breathed.' *2 Timothy 3:16*

[a]The Bible claims to be the word of God.
> 'For prophecy never had its origin in the will of man, but men spoke from God ...' *2 Peter 1:21*

"So where is the evidence to support such massive claims?"

TWO TESTS
You can give the Bible, or any other book, two tests to see if it is truthful.

To a skeptic these tests many not be absolute "proof" of the divine inspiration of the Bible, but they do show if the Bible may be relied on.

TEST ONE: THE TEST OF EXTERNAL EVIDENCE
Here, two sources confirm the reliability of the Bible as a trustworthy historical document: archaeology and early non-Christian writers.

1. ARCHAEOLOGY
A Jewish archaeologist
Nelson Glueck has said, "It may be stated categorically that no archaeological discovery has ever controverted a biblical reference. Scores of archaeological findings have been made which confirm in clear outline or exact detail historical statements in the Bible."

Sir William Ramsey
Sir William Ramsey, one of the greatest archaeologists of all time, showed that Luke made no mistakes in references to 32 countries, 54 cities, and 9 islands.

2. THE TESTIMONY OF NON-CHRISTIAN WRITERS
Two first-century Roman writers of the period tell us about him: Tacitus, c. 55 – c. AD 120, (*Annals 15.44*) and Pliny the Younger, c. AD 62 – c.114 (*Letters 10.96*).

Flavius Josephus
Next to the Bible in importance, the works of Jewish historian Flavius Josephus, AD 37-95, are the

most authoritative ancient source for illuminating the people, places, and events recorded in the Old and New Testaments. He was born in Jerusalem only four years after Jesus' crucifixion.

In his book *Jewish Antiquities, 18:63*, Josephus records: "About this time lived Jesus, a wise man, if indeed one ought to call him a man. For he was the achiever of extraordinary deeds and was a teacher of those who accept the truth gladly. He won over many Jews and many of the Greeks. He was the Messiah. When he was indicted by the principal men among us and Pilate condemned him to be crucified, those who had come to love him originally did not cease to do so; for he appeared to them on the third day restored to life, as the prophets of the Deity had foretold these and countless other marvelous things about him. And the tribe of Christians, so named after him, has not disappeared to this day."

Eighteen non-Christian sources can be traced back to the first century

Dr. G.R. Habermas has discovered that within 110 years of Christ's crucifixion, eighteen non-Christian sources mention more than "one hundred facts, beliefs, and teachings from the life of Christ and early Christendom. These items, I might add, mention almost every major detail of Jesus' life, including miracles, the Resurrection, and His claims to deity."

TEST TWO: THE TEST OF INTERNAL EVIDENCE

This refers to evidence within the Bible itself.

The internal evidence test reveals just how consistent the Bible is. It would be expected that a collection of: 66 books,
written by over 40 authors,
in 3 languages,
on 3 continents,
over a span of 1,500 years,
covering hundreds of controversial subjects could hardly have single theme.

Yet all the authors of the Bible write about one theme – God's redemption of humankind.

A QUOTE TO CHEW OVER

"I set out to look for truth on the borderland where Greece and Asia meet, and found it there. You may press the words of Luke in a degree beyond any other historian's and they stand the keenest scrutiny and the hardest treatment." *Sir William Ramsay*

"Is the Bible accurate and historically reliable?"

WHAT'S THE PROBLEM?
"Is it historically reliable? Is every doctrine in the Bible to be believed? All human beings make mistakes. How can Christians insist that the Bible is trustworthy?"

What the Bible is not
• The Bible is not primarily a history book. Yes, it does contain a great deal of history, especially about the Jews, but biblical writers were highly selective in the subjects they chose to cover.
• The Bible is not a scientific book. Yes, it does deal with the creation of the world, which eminent scientists accept, but the Bible does not answer the question "How was the world made?" so much as the questions "Who made the world/and why?"
• The Bible is not primarily a work of great literature. Yes, it does contain many highly acclaimed writings, such as the book of Job which Tennyson called "the greatest poem of ancient and modern times," but the Bible was not meant to be read as wonderful literature.

Accuracy of the Bible
Archaeologists have discovered hundreds of thousands of ancient writings, and have deciphered inscriptions on walls and stones. Some of these go back to the second millennium BC.

What is the purpose of the Bible?
Even though the Bible consists of 66 books it has a one theme: salvation.

Two examples of prophecies given hundreds of of years before Jesus' birth in Bethlehem:

• **Life**
"But you, Bethlehem Ephrathah,
    though you are small among the
    clans of Judah,
out of you will come for me
    one who will be ruler over Israel,
whose origins are from old,
    from ancient times."
    Micah 5:2

• **Death**
"They divide my garments among
    them
    and cast lots for my clothing."
    Psalm 22:18

The Bible does not give a contradictory message on this subject. The life and death of Jesus remarkably fulfils the Old Testament prophecies.

Key verse in the Bible about the Bible's infallibility
All scripture is God-breathed and is useful for teaching, rebuking, correcting and training in righteousness, so that the man of God may be thoroughly equipped for every good work.
2 Timothy 3:16-17

WHAT'S THE CONCLUSION?
The experience of men and women throughout the centuries confirms the fact that the message of the Bible is consistent and trustworthy.

Approach the Bible with reverence:

"I began to read the holy scriptures upon my knees, laying aside all other books, and praying over, if possible every line and word. This proved meat indeed and drink to my soul. I daily received fresh life, light and power from above." *George Whitefield*

A QUOTE TO CHEW OVER
"Let us therefore yield ourselves and bow to the authority of the Holy Scriptures, which can neither err nor deceive."
Augustine of Hippo

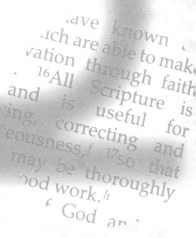

"Is every word of the Bible literally true?"

WHAT'S THE PROBLEM?
"How literalistic do you have to be?! Surely much of the Bible needs to be taken with a pinch of salt."

It's easy to misquote and apply the Bible in a forced way
In a film some years ago, Peter Sellers played the part of a clergyman. He knocked at one door and was confronted by an aggressive woman who asked him, "Do you believe everything in the Bible?" "Yes," replied the clergyman. "Then here are two quotes for you," bellowed the woman. "Judas went out and hanged himself." And, "Go and do thou likewise." Then she slammed the door.

Look at the context
In the book of Job the first 37 chapters record the dialogue between Job and his three so-called "comforters".

Most of what they say is recorded to be contradicted, not to be believed and acted on.

God tells them off for what they said: "The Lord … said to Eliphaz the Temanite, 'I am angry with you and your two friends, because you have not spoken of me what is right, as my servant Job has." *Job 42:7*

The whole book of Job is the word of God. But it is not right to pick a phrase from the first 37 chapters of the book and declare: "This is the word of God," for it may not be. The first 37 chapters have to be read in the light of the last five chapters.

Observe the literary style
• Is it anthropomorphic?
• Is it a description of God deliberately represented in a human form?

God is sometimes depicted as having eyes, nostrils, ears, an outstretched arm, hands, fingers and a mouth. He is even pictured as having wings. "Under his (God's) wings you will find refuge." *Psalm 91:4*

Such pictures were never meant to be taken literally. The metaphor of a bird is used to illustrate God's loving protection. His outstretched arm denotes his power to save.

14

Is it poetic?

When the psalmist in Psalm 19:6 says that the sun "rises at one end of the heavens" he is not giving us a scientific lesson which disproves what Galileo taught. He is just using poetic imagery to describe the brilliance of the sun. "For the sun ... is like a bridegroom coming forth from his pavilion." *Psalm 19:5*

Is it symbolic?

A symbol is an object, or number, or creature used to represent an idea, fact or person. When in the book of Revelation John talked of seeing a "Lamb", he was referring to Jesus. In Revelation specific numbers are often used as symbols.

What is the viewpoint and purpose?

Several people recording the same event will often choose to tell different, true details because their purposes and angles differ.

What about verbal inspiration?

Christians believe that the Bible was not just inspired by God in a general way but that this inspiration extended to the actual words used by the human authors.

The apostle Paul claimed that what God had revealed to him he communicated to others by God's Spirit and not by human wisdom.

"This is what we speak, not in words taught us by human wisdom but in words taught by the Spirit, expressing spiritual truths in spiritual words." *1 Corinthians 2:13*

A QUOTE TO CHEW OVER

"Our claim is that God has revealed himself by speaking; that this divine (or God-breathed) speech has been written down and preserved in Scripture; and that Scripture is, in fact, God's word written, which therefore is true and reliable and has divine authority over men." *John Stott*

"How can only one interpretation of the Bible be correct?"

WHAT'S THE PROBLEM?
"You interpret the Bible in one way, I interpret the Bible in another way. Who's to say who is right?"

Hermeneutics: the science of interpreting Scripture
Whether studying a whole Bible book, a particular passage of Scripture, or a single verse there are certain principles of interpretation which help us come to understand what the Bible is saying. These principles are called hermeneutics.

I. PRAY FOR THE HELP OF GOD'S HOLY SPIRIT
"When the Spirit of truth comes, he will guide you into all truth," said Jesus to his friends.
John 16:12

2. LOOK FOR THE NATURAL SENSE OF THE PASSAGE
Many parts of the Bible are intended to be taken literally, but others are figurative. The natural meaning of a passage will not always mean the literal meaning of a passage. How can you tell which is which?
- Consider first the context of the passage – what precedes it and what follows it?
- Then consider the natural sense of the passage.
- Use your common sense.
- Keep in mind what the original writer had in mind and the needs of the people to whom he was writing.

God has spoken
God's nature is to reveal himself. "God is light; in him there is no darkness at all."
1 John 1:5
   In Scripture God has spoken and spoken in such a way that he intends us to understand what he has said.

3. INTERPRET SCRIPTURE WITH SCRIPTURE

How are we to interpret verses from "apocalyptic" Bible books where strange images are used to portray hidden truths?

How would you set about interpreting the following verse?

> "These are they who have come out of the great tribulation; they have washed their robes and made them white in the blood of the Lamb." *Revelation 7:14*

Ask the following question: "Is there an image here to be visualized or a symbol to be interpreted?"

Then try to discover what each part of the symbol means in the rest of the Bible.

A. What do "white robes" stand for?

Revelation 22:14 says, "Blessed are those who wash their robes, that they may have the right to the tree of life."

So white robes refer to the righteousness of God's people.

B. What does the "blood of the Lamb" stand for?

John 1:29 has John the Baptist saying about Jesus, "Look, the Lamb of God, who takes away the sin of the world!"

So the blood of the Lamb refers to the death of Jesus.

C. What does "washed" stand for?

1 Corinthians 6:11, referring to Christians, says, "You were washed."

So people who have been washed refers to people who have placed their trust in Jesus and have been cleansed from their sin.

WHAT'S THE CONCLUSION?

"Let us know, then, that the true meaning of Scripture is the natural and obvious meaning; and let us embrace and abide by it resolutely. Let us not only neglect as doubtful, but boldly set aside as deadly corruptions those pretended expositions which lead us away from the natural meaning." *John Calvin*

A QUOTE TO CHEW OVER

Never "expound one place of Scripture that it be repugnant to another." *The Thirty-Nine Articles, Article XX, Of the authority of the Church.*

"Why do Christians disagree among themselves about so many things in the Bible?"

WHAT'S THE PROBLEM?
"There seem to be so many things about which Christians come to divergent conclusions, as they read the same Bible. They can't all be led by the Holy Spirit, as so many of them claim."

WHAT ARE SOME OF THE ISSUES THAT CHRISTIANS DIFFER OVER?

Women
Should women be allowed to hold positions of leadership in the church?

Evolution
Can a Christian believe in any form of evolution?

Baptism
Should you be baptized as a believer or is it okay as a baby?

Form of Baptism
Is immersion in water the only form or is sprinkling acceptable?

Tongues
Should all Christians speak in tongues or have tongues ceased?

Gifts of the Holy Spirit
Should all the gifts of the Spirit be used in every Christian fellowship?

Eternal security
Can a Christian who has turned his back on God lose his salvation?

Predestination
Has God already determined who is going to heaven?

Israel
Should we believe that the Old Testament prophecies about Israel will be literally fulfilled?

Church government
Should it be a centralized hierarchy or run entirely at the local level?

Miracles
Should we expect to find all kinds of miracles in our local fellowships today or did they end with the apostles?

The millennium
Is the thousand year reign of Christ to be taken literally as a future event on this earth, or symbolically as a present spiritual reality?

Pacificism
Should Christians be pacifists or is fighting for your country part of God's will?

WHAT TO DO ABOUT THESE DIFFERENCES

1. Distinguish between what is a fundamental undisputed truth taught in the Bible and disputed points of secondary importance, over which Christians form divergent views.

2. Pray and try to come to a reasoned view about what the Bible teaches on each topic.

3. Try to see the biblical reasons for a viewpoint with which you differ. If you were brought up believing in infant baptism, think about reasons why many Christians feel that immersion in water is the only way.

4. Come to an understanding of the measure of God's grace, that is, that grace is God's essential character as he deals with our shortcomings.

5. Try not to argue about differing views.

"Truth suffers more by the heat of its defenders than from the arguments of its opposers."
William Penn

WHAT'S THE CONCLUSION?

Different viewpoints in themselves are not necessarily a problem:

"One man considers one day more sacred than another; another man considers every day alike. Each one should be fully convinced in his own mind. He who regards one day as special, does so to the Lord. He who eats meat, eats to the Lord, for he gives thanks to God; and he who abstains, does so to the Lord and gives thanks to God."
Romans 14:5-6

"Who are you to judge someone else's servant? To his own master he stands or falls."
Romans 14:4

A QUOTE TO CHEW OVER

"In fundamentals unity, in non-fundamentals liberty, in all things charity."
Rupert Meldenius

"Isn't the Bible only believed by the old, the unintelligent and the gullible?"

WHAT'S THE PROBLEM?
"The Bible was OK for previous centuries. But now that we are better educated we can see that the Bible is just a collection of myths and stories which cannot stand up to the scrutiny of scholarly investigation."

ARE THERE ANY SCHOLARS WHO STILL BELIEVE IN THE INTEGRITY OF THE BIBLE?

The testimony of one of the most respected scholars of Oriental studies:
"The reader may rest assured that nothing has been found by archaeologist to disturb a reasonable faith, and nothing has been discovered which can disprove a single theological doctrine. We no longer trouble ourselves with attempts to 'harmonize' religion and science, or to 'prove' the Bible. The Bible can stand for itself."
Professor William F. Albright

The testimony of probably the most qualified Old Testament linguist of all time:
"For forty-five years continuously, since I left college, I have devoted myself to the one great study of the Old Testament, in all its languages, in all its archaeology, in all its translations, and as far as possible in everything bearing upon its text and history.
"The result of my forty-five years of study of the Bible has led me all the time to a firmer faith that in the Old Testament we have a true historical account of the Israelite people." *Dr Robert Dick Wilson*

The testimony of a scientific archaeologist and student of ancient classical history and literature
"Luke is a historian of the first rank; not merely are his statements of fact trustworthy; he is possessed of the true historic sense. He seizes the important and critical events and shows their true nature at greater length. In short, this author should be placed along with the very greatest of historians."
Sir William Ramsay

20

CROSS CHECK WITH THE GREATEST ROMAN HISTORIAN IN THE DAYS OF THE EMPIRE.

It was widely rumored that the great fire of Rome in AD 64 had been instigated by Nero so that he could be credited with its rebuilding. Tacitus, in his history of the reign of Nero, incidentally confirms the central event of the New Testament as an accepted historical fact.

> "Therefore, to scotch the rumor, Nero substituted as culprits, and punished with the utmost refinements of cruelty, a class of men, loathed for their vices, whom the crowd styled as Christians. Christus, from whom they got their name, had been executed by sentence of the procurator Pontius Pilate when Tiberius was emperor." *Cornelius Tacitus*

WHAT'S THE CONCLUSION?

There is a golden Key that will unlock the mysteries of the Bible to anyone who uses it. It will open the vault of God's inexhaustible treasure of truth. The Lord Jesus Christ is the golden Key. He makes the Bible an open book.

> "My purpose is that they may be encouraged in heart and united in love, so that they may have the full riches of complete understanding, in order that they may know the mystery of God, namely, Christ, in whom are hidden all the treasures of wisdom and knowledge." *Colossians 2:2-3*

A QUOTE TO CHEW OVER

> "We cannot rely on the doctrine of Scripture until we are absolutely convinced that God is its author." *John Calvin*

"Isn't the God of the Old Testament different from the God of the New Testament?"

WHAT'S THE PROBLEM?

"Do we have to bother about the Old Testament? Can't we just stick to the New Testament and the Christian God of the New Testament?"

The links between the Old Testament (O.T.) and the New Testament (N.T.)

In the writings of:	Direct quotations from the O.T.	O.T. incidents	O.T. allusions mentioned
Paul	132	38	13
James	4	3	1
Peter	10	5	8

JESUS IS THE ULTIMATE FOCUS OF EVERY OLD TESTAMENT BOOK

Bible book	Jesus is seen as	O.T. reference	N.T. reference
Genesis	The offspring of the woman	Genesis 3:15	Galatians 4:4
Exodus	Bread	Exodus 16:11-35	John 6:32-35
Leviticus	Our Great High Priest	Leviticus 21	Hebrews 4:14
Numbers	Rock	Numbers 20:11	1 Corinthians 10:4
Deuteronomy	Prophet	Deuteronomy 18:15-19	Acts 3:22-23
Joshua	Joshua is seen as a type of Jesus		
Judges	Our Deliverer	Judges 3:9	
Ruth	Our Kinsman-redeemer	Ruth 2:1	
1 & 2 Samuel	The descendant of David		Romans 1:3-4
1 & 2 Kings	King of kings and Lord of lords		
1 & 2 Chronicles	King of kings and Lord of lords		
Ezra & Nehemiah	Lord of heaven and earth		
Esther	Our Esther-advocate		
Job	Our Hedge	Job 1:10	Colossians 3:3
Psalms	Our all in all		Colossians 1:17-19
Proverbs	The Wisdom of God	Proverbs 8:12	1 Corinthians 1:30

The opening verse of the New Testament

"A record of the genealogy of Jesus Christ the son of David, the son of Abraham." *Matthew 1:1*

Through four groups of 14 Old Testament people Matthew traces Jesus' line back to Abraham.

The purpose of the Old and New Testaments

The Old Testament shows human rebellion, God's continual loving deliverance of his people, God's holiness and justice and his people's inability to keep God's law.

The New Testament shows God's solution to the human dilemma revealed in the Old Testament – a solution which is often foreshadowed at in the Old Testament.

A QUOTE TO CHEW OVER

"Every word of the Bible rings with Christ." *Martin Luther*

Bible book	Jesus is seen as	O.T. reference	N.T. reference
Ecclesiastes	The Creator	Ecclesiastes 12:1	John 1:1-3
Song of Songs	The heavenly Bridegroom	Song of Songs 5:10	
Isaiah	The divine Substitute	Isaiah 53:5	1 Peter 2:24
Jeremiah	The Hope of Israel	Jeremiah 14:8	
Lamentations	My Portion	Lamentations 3:24	
Ezekiel	The Shepherd	Ezekiel 34:23	John 10:11-13
Daniel	Son of man	Daniel 7:13	
Hosea	Lord God of hosts	Hosea 12:5	
Joel	The Hope of his people	Joel 3:16	
Amos	The God of hosts	Amos 4:13	
Obadiah	The Lord of the kingdom	v. 21	
Jonah	The risen Prophet		Matthew 12:39-41
Micah	The Ruler in Israel	Micah 5:2	
Nahum	A Refuge	Nahum 1:7	
Habakkuk	The Man who justifies by faith	Habakkuk 2:4	Acts 13:38-39
Zephaniah	Israel's King	Zephaniah 3:15	
Haggai	The Desire of all nations		Haggai 2:7
Zechariah	The Branch – our Servant	Zechariah 3:8	Mark 10:45
Malachi	Sun of Righteousness	Malachi 4:2	

"The Gospels seem to be OK, but why read the rest of the New Testament?"

WHAT'S THE PROBLEM?

"Outside the Gospels everything seems to be so out of date. And anyway, the New Testament was written by very different types of people: a converted Jewish theologian, a Gentile doctor, a fisherman. There's even one book, the book of Hebrews, by an unknown author."

Paul's letters

Many of Paul's letters were written before the Gospels. They reveal the work of the Spirit as he led the early Christians into all truth. *See John 16:13.*

Divine inspiration is responsible for unity

The only way the unity between the 39 books of the Old Testament and the 27 New Testament books can be satisfactorily explained is that they are all divinely inspired. Each writer was guided by the Spirit of God.

Paul wrote that he thanked God continually "because, when you received the word of God, which you heard from us, you accepted it not as the word of men, but as it actually is, the word of God, which is at work in you who believe."

1 Thessalonians 2:13

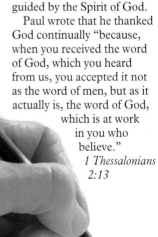

JESUS IS THE ULTIMATE FOCUS
OF EVERY NEW TESTAMENT BOOK

Bible book	Jesus is seen as	N.T. Bible reference
Matthew	King of the Jews	Matthew 2:2
Mark	God's righteous Servant	Mark 10:45
Luke	The Man for everyone	Luke 19:10
John	God's one and only Son	John 1:14, 18
Acts	Our ascended Lord	Acts 1:2, 10-11
Romans	The Lord our Righteousness	Romans 10:4
1 Corinthians	The first fruits of the dead	1 Corinthians 15:20
2 Corinthians	Our Competence	2 Corinthians 3:5
Galatians	Our Liberator	Galatians 1:4; 5:1
Ephesians	The Head of the Church	Ephesians 1:22; 5:23
Philippians	Our Strength	Philippians 4:13
Colossians	The fulness of the Deity	Colossians 2:9
1 Thessalonians	Our coming Lord	1 Thessalonians 1:10; 4:16-17
2 Thessalonians	Our soon expected coming Lord	2 Thessalonians 1–2
1 Timothy	The Mystery of godliness	1 Timothy 3:16
2 Timothy	Our righteous Judge	2 Timothy 4:1
Titus	Great God and Savior	Titus 2:10-11; 3:4, 6
Philemon	The Restorer of relationships	Philemon 15-16
Hebrews	Our Apostle and high priest	Hebrews 3:1
James	The Lord who comes near	James 4:8
1 Peter	The suffering Lamb	1 Peter 1:19; 2:21
2 Peter	The Lord of Glory	2 Peter 3:18
1 John	The Son of God	1 John 3:8
2 John	The Truth	2 John v. 2
3 John	The Name	3 John v. 7
Jude	Our Savior	Jude v. 25
Revelation	The victorious Savior	Revelation 1:18

A QUOTE TO CHEW OVER

"Knowledge of scripture is knowledge of Christ and ignorance of them is ignorance of him." *Jerome*

"Isn't the Old Testament unreliable?"

WHAT'S THE PROBLEM?
"All the books of the Old Testament were written thousands of years ago. We can't possibly know that what we now have is the same as the original writing."

Before 1947
Before 1947 the earliest manuscript of the Hebrew Old Testament in the possession of scholars was dated AD 826. That is over 1,000 years after the last book of the Old Testament was written.

Bible scholars would have dearly loved to have older manuscripts of the Old Testament so that they could compare them with each other. But nobody thought such ancient manuscripts existed, because these manuscripts would have rotted in the sun, wind and rain.

Enter the Dead Sea Scrolls
In 1947 a young Bedouin shepherd found some jars filled with ancient rolls of leather in a cave near the Dead Sea. He had no idea that he had stumbled on the greatest discovery of biblical archaeology of the twentieth century!

One thousand years older
Archaeologists were quick to point out that these scrolls formed the library of a religious community that lived at Qumran near the Dead Sea.

Eventually they discovered over 500 documents. 100 of these scrolls contain material from the Old Testament. There are verses or chapters from every book of the Bible except Esther.

The Isaiah scroll dates back to about 100 BC. It is now the oldest manuscript of a complete book of the Old Testament.

These Hebrew scrolls are 1,000 years older than all previously known manuscripts of the Hebrew Bible.

Are they accurate?

Bible scholars painstakingly compared the Dead Sea Scrolls with the text of AD 826, written 1,000 years later. They were amazed at the accuracy of these scrolls. The texts were almost identical.

The differences were so slight they are hardly worth mentioning. For example in Isaiah 45:2 the Dead Sea Scrolls say "hills straight", while the King James Version (a descendant of the previous earliest-known texts) reads "crooked places straight." In Isaiah 45:8 the Dead Sea Scrolls say "rain down righteous", while the King James Version reads "pour down righteousness."

Not one truth of the Christian faith in these scrolls differs from the Bible translations we use today.

WHAT'S THE CONCLUSION?

The texts we have of the Old Testament are most reliable.

A QUOTE TO CHEW OVER

"All men are like grass, and all their glory is like the flowers of the field; the grass withers and the flowers fall, but the word of the Lord stands for ever." *1 Peter 1:24-25*

"Why bother with Old Testament?"

WHAT'S THE PROBLEM?
"These musty books were written so long ago they can hardly have anything to say to us in the 21st century."

The 39 books which make up the Old Testament were all written well over 2,000 years ago. Some may been written as early as 2000 BC, making them about 4,000 years old.

Old is not necessarily useless
Many works of literature which are still considered great today date back thousands of years.

What matters is their content and not their age.

Bible prophecy

The Old Testament prophets spoke and wrote the messages they had received from God.

"Prophecy (in the Old Testament) never had its origin in the will of man, but men spoke from God as they were carried along by the Holy Spirit." *2 Peter 1:21*

The Old Testament looked beyond itself to a time in the future when God would provide salvation for the human race.

PROPHECIES ABOUT JESUS IN THE OLD TESTAMENT

	Prophecy about the Messiah	Fulfilled by Jesus
1	Born of a virgin *Isaiah 7:14*	*Matthew 1:23*
2	God's special messenger would precede the Messiah *Malachi 3:1*	*Luke 3:4, 15-18*
3	The Messiah to be born in Bethlehem *Micah 5:2*	*Matthew 2:6*
4	The Messiah to be anointed by the Spirit *Isaiah 11:1-2*	*Matthew 3:16*
5	The Redeemer would come riding on a young donkey *Zechariah 9:9*	*Mark 11:1-11*
6	God's Servant would be rejected *Isaiah 53:3*	*Luke 18:31-33; 23:13-25*
7	The Messiah would be mocked *Psalm 22:1-8*	*Luke 23:35*
8	The Messiah's clothing would be divided up by lot *Psalm 22:18*	*Matthew 27:35*
9	No bones of the Messiah would be broken *Psalm 34:20*	*John 19:32-33,36*
10	The Messiah would be pierced *Zechariah 12:10*	*John 19:34*

Jesus "bothered" with the Old Testament
• He is recorded as quoting from it.
• The Old Testament book from which he quoted most often was Psalms.
• He referred to over 20 Old Testament people.

WHAT'S THE CONCLUSION?
Jesus quoted the Old Testament when tempted as well as when he died on the cross. What greater reason could we have for trusting the Old Testament?

A QUOTE TO CHEW OVER
"In the Old Testament the New is concealed.
In the New Testament the Old is revealed."
Augustine of Hippo

"Is the Bible a reliable book of genuine divine prophecy?"

WHAT'S THE PROBLEM?
"How do the prophecies in the Old Testament tie in with what happened in the New Testament? Can't you just explain away all the so-called prophecies?"

The prophecies about Jesus
The Bible contains hundreds of detailed prophecies.

Over 60 prophecies in the Old Testament are distinct predictions about Jesus.

Some of these prophecies were made 1,000 years before Jesus lived his life on earth.

Many of these prophecies concern Jesus' crucifixion. These prophecies were made over 500 years before crucifixion was first used anywhere in the world as a form of capital punishment.

Could it just be a fluke that Jesus fulfilled all these prophecies?
A scientist picked out 48 such prophecies and determined that the probability of one man randomly fulfilling them all is 1 in 10 to the exponent of 157. That is 1 followed by 157 zeros!

10,000,000,000,000,000,000,000,000,000,000,000,000,000,000,000,000,
000,000,000,000,000,000,000,000,000,000,000,000,000,000,000,000,000,
000,000,000,000,000,000,000,000,000,000,000,000,000,000,000,000,000,
000,000,000,000

Your chances of winning a typical lottery jackpot is about 1 in 108,000,000. Yet, Jesus fulfilled all the prophecies.

OLD TESTAMENT PROPHECIES ABOUT JESUS' BIRTH

	Prophesied	Fulfilled
1	Born as a descendant of a woman, *Genesis 3:15*	*Galatians 4:4*
2	Born of a virgin, *Isaiah 7:14*	*Matthew 1:18-25*
3	Born as a descendant of David, *Jeremiah 23:5*	*Luke 3:31*
4	Born in Bethlehem, *Micah 5:2*	*Matthew 2:1-6*
5.	Herod kills the children, *Jeremiah 31:15*	*Matthew 2:16-18*

OLD TESTAMENT PROPHECIES ABOUT JESUS' DEATH

	Prophesied	Fulfilled
1	Betrayed by a friend, *Psalm 41:9*	*John 13:18-27*
2	Sold for 30 pieces of silver, *Zechariah 11:12*	*Matthew 26:14-15*
3	Forsaken by his disciples, *Zechariah 13:7*	*Mark 14:27, 50*
4	Accused by false witnesses, *Psalm 35:11, 20-21*	*Matthew 26:59-61*
5	Silent before accusers, *Isaiah 53:7*	*Matthew 27:12-14*
6	Wounded and bruised, *Isaiah 53:4-6*	*1 Peter 2:21-25*
7	Beaten and spat on, *Isaiah 50:6*	*Matthew 26:67-68*
8	Mocked, *Psalm 22:6-8*	*Matthew 27:27-31*
9	Hands and feet pierced, *Psalm 22:16*	*John 20:24-28*
10	Crucified with thieves, *Isaiah 53:12*	*Matthew 27:38*
11	Prayed for his enemies, *Isaiah 53:12*	*Luke 23:34*
12	People shake their heads, *Psalm 22:7; 109:25*	*Matthew 27:39*
13	Cloths gambled for, *Psalm 22:18*	*John 19:23-24*
14	Became very thirsty, *Psalm 22:15*	*John 19:28*
15	Gall and vinegar offered to him, *Psalm 69:21*	*Matthew 27:34*
16	His forsaken cry, *Psalm 22:1*	*Matthew 27:46*
17	Committed himself to God, *Psalm 31:5*	*Luke 23:46*
18	Bones not broken, *Psalm 34:20*	*John 19:32-36*
19	His side pierced, *Zechariah 12:10*	*John 19:34, 37*
20	Buried in rich man's tomb, *Isaiah 53:9*	*Matthew 27:57-60*

WHAT'S THE CONCLUSION?

"Concerning this salvation, the prophets, who spoke of the grace that was to come to you, searched intently and with the greatest care, trying to find out the time and circumstances to which the Spirit of Christ in them was pointing when he predicted the sufferings of Christ and the glories that would follow." *1 Peter 1:10-11*

A QUOTE TO CHEW OVER

"Jesus said, 'Did not the Christ have to suffer these things and then enter his glory?' And beginning with Moses and all the Prophets, he explained to them what was said in all the Scriptures concerning himself." *Luke 24:26-27*

"Did Adam and Eve really exist?"

WHAT'S THE PROBLEM?
"Are we still meant to believe in the 'myth' of Adam and Eve? If so, what about the snake or serpent in the garden of Eden? Do we have to believe in him as well?"

Look for biblical answers
Understanding the Bible is not a question of: What answer most satisfies me?

Understanding the Bible is a matter of making sure that our beliefs are in line with the overall teaching of Scripture. This will mean that we should be certain about some things, but may have to remain uncertain or reverently skeptical about other things.

Adam and Eve: did they exist?
The question to ask is, "Does the Bible teach that they existed?"

Were Adam and Eve literal people? For many Christians the clinching Bible passage is Romans 5:12-21.

Note the disobedience of Adam. This meant that sin and death came into the world.

"Therefore, just as sin entered the world through one man (Adam), and death through sin, and in this way death came to all men, because all sinned . . ." *Romans 5:12*

Note how Adam's disobedience is contrasted with the obedience of Jesus which leads to forgiveness and salvation.

"Consequently, just as the result of one trespass was condemnation for all men, so also the result of one act of righteousness was justification that brings life for all men. For just as through the disobedience of the one man the many were made sinners, so also through the obedience of the one man the many will be made righteous." *Romans 5:18-19*

Paul's teaching

To Paul, Adam and Eve clearly existed.

If Adam and Eve were not real people in history his whole comparison between them and Jesus breaks down.

The serpent: did he exist?

The question to ask is, "Does the Bible teach that a serpent or Satan existed?"

The serpent of the first book of the Bible pops up again in the last book of the Bible.

In the book of Revelation the serpent is obviously portrayed in a symbolic way. No serpent which ever existed managed to spew out enough water from its mouth to form a river.

"The great dragon was hurled down – that ancient serpent called the devil, or Satan, who leads the whole world astray. ... Then from his mouth the serpent spewed water like a river, to overtake the woman and sweep her away with the torrent." *Revelation 12:9, 15*

From this it is fair to conclude that Satan is depicted in the form of a serpent. There is no reason not to believe that Satan appeared to Adam and Eve in this symbolic form.

BY WAY OF ILLUSTRATION
Mary Queen of Scots once asked John Knox, "Ye interpret the Scriptures in one manner, and they [the Pope and his Cardinals] in another; whom shall I believe, and who shall judge?"

John Knox replied: "Believe God, who plainly speaks in his Word: and beyond what the Word teaches you, you should not believe either the one or the other. The Word of God is plain in itself; and if it appears to be obscure in one place, the Holy Spirit, who never contradicts himself, explains it more clearly in other places."

"Why is the Bible so against witchcraft?"

WHAT'S THE PROBLEM?
"What's the big problem about witches? After all, witchcraft is a legal religion in the United States. And 'white witches' claim to use their magic for good purposes."

What is witchcraft?

"Magic is universal and may be 'black' or 'white'.

"Black magic attempts to produce evil results through such methods as curses, spells, destruction of models of one's enemy and alliance with evil spirits. It often takes the form of witchcraft.

"White magic tries to undo curses and spells and to use occult forces for the good of oneself and others. There is no doubt that magic and sorcery are not always mere superstition, but have a reality behind them."
K.A. Kitchen, Dictionary of the Bible, IVP

What does the Old Testament say about the realm of the occult?

The Scriptures condemn sorcery. All sorcery stands opposed to a proper sense of dependence upon God.

"Then Joseph said to them, 'Do not interpretations belong to God?'" *Genesis 40:8*

"Let no one be found among you who sacrifices his son or daughter in the fire, who practices divination or sorcery, interprets omens, engages in witchcraft, or casts spells, or who is a medium or spiritist or who consults the dead. Anyone who does these things is detestable to the Lord." *Deuteronomy 18:10-12*

THE WITCH OF ENDOR

Witches are supposed to have the ability to manipulate evil powers by magic.

The witch of Endor, 1 Samuel 28, was a medium who claimed contact with the spirit world. King Saul knew that it was wrong to consult mediums. He had even outlawed them, yet he went and consulted the witch of Endor. For this Saul stood guilty before God.

SAUL'S EPITAPH

"Saul died because he was unfaithful to the Lord; he did not keep the word of the Lord, and even consulted a medium for guidance, and did not enquire of the Lord."
1 Chronicles 10:13-14

What does the New Testament say about witchcraft?

Witchcraft is listed as being one of the acts of the sinful nature:

"The acts of sinful nature are obvious: sexual immorality, impurity and debauchery; idolatry and witchcraft . . ."
Galatians 5:19-20

The book of Revelation condemns sorcery in the strongest terms:

"But the cowardly, the unbelieving, the vile, the murderers, the sexually immoral, those who practice magic arts, the idolaters and all liars – their place will be in the fiery lake of burning sulphur." *Revelation 21:8*

"Outside are the dogs, those who practice magic arts … and everyone who loves and practices falsehood."
Revelation 22:15

WHAT'S THE CONCLUSION?

"You must be blameless before the Lord your God."
Deuteronomy 18:9-13

A QUOTE TO CHEW OVER

"Magic is a rival to true religion." *K.A. Kitchen*

"Isn't the story of Jonah and the whale no more than a fishy tale?"

WHAT'S THE PROBLEM?
"Surely this story must be thought of as just a legend. Even if you could find a fish big enough to swallow you, how could you survive three days in its digestive tract and then escape alive?"

Jesus and Jonah
Jesus referred to this as an historical event. He pointed to it as a foreshadowing of his own death and resurrection.

Jonah is the only prophet Jesus likened to himself: *Matthew 12:39-41*

Three days and three nights
The Hebrew idiom "three days and three nights" only requires a part of the first and third days.

WHAT FISH IS FEATURED IN THE BOOK OF JONAH?

We are not told.

Was it a whale? The translation in the King James Version (A.V.) of the word as "whale" is not accurate. The translation "a great fish" is better.

Jesus never said the fish was a whale, but "a huge fish," *Matthew 12:40*.

Was it a "Sea Dog"? The "Sea Dog" (*Carcharodon carcharias*) is found in warm seas and can reach a length of 40 feet.

Was it a sperm whale? Sperm whales can swallow lumps of food eight feet in diameter. Entire skeletons of sharks up to 16 feet have been found in them.

Can a person survive being swallowed by a fish?
There are several documented accounts of people who have been swallowed by whales and large fish and have survived. Some of these accounts appear to be rather extraordinary.

One reports that in 1758, a sailor fell overboard in the Mediterranean and was swallowed by a sea dog. The captain of the vessel ordered a cannon to be fired at the fish which, after it was hit, vomited up the sailor alive and unharmed! Another account states that in 1891, James Bartley, a sailor aboard the whaling ship Star of the East, was swallowed by a whale in the vicinity of the Falkland Islands. The whale was harpooned and brought aboard the whaling ship. Inside and still alive was the sailor, though he had been imprisoned within the whale for more than 48 hours. It took the sailor two weeks to recover.

WHAT'S THE CONCLUSION?
The truth of Jonah and the great fish does not hang on our understanding of how this event could have occurred. Why could not the God of creation directly use his creation for a special purpose?

"How are we able to know if we can trust the existing New Testament?"

WHAT'S THE PROBLEM?
"Can we trust the New Testament documents? Could it not have been tampered with over the ages? How does the documentary evidence for the New Testament stand the test when compared with the documentary evidence for other ancient writings?"

Greatest number of manuscripts

There are more manuscripts of the Bible than any other single book from the ancient world. More than 25,000 manuscripts of portions of the New Testament exist. Many of these are comparatively early manuscripts; other classical works typically have 1200–1400 years separating the original writing and surviving manuscript copies.

When the surviving manuscripts about other ancient events are ccompared with the surviving Bible manuscripts, it is seen just how good the Bible manuscripts are. Nobody doubts that Julius Caesar invaded Britain, but there are only 10 ancient manuscript copies that confirm this. The earliest copy was made about 800 years after the event.

THE BIBLE'S AUTHENTICITY compared with the authenticity of other ancient writings

Author/Writing	Date Written	Earliest Copy	Gap/Time span	No. of Copies
Caesar's *Gallic Wars*	100–44 BC	AD 900	950 years	10
Plato's *Tetralogies*	427–347 BC	AD 900	1,250 years	7
Tacitus	AD 100	AD 1100	1,000 years	20
Thucydides	460–400 BC	AD 900	1,400 years	8
Sophocles	496–406 BC	AD 1000	1,400 years	100
Aristotle	384–322 BC	AD 1100	1,400 years	5
New Testament	AD 40–100	AD 130 AD 350 (full manuscript)		5,000 Greek 10,000 Latin 9,000 Others

Differences between the manuscripts of the New Testament

Because the New Testament writings were so important, scribes took great care when copying them. The differences are minor ones.

No single doctrine hangs on a disputed reading.

WHAT'S THE CONCLUSION?

"In the variety and fullness of the evidence on which it rests, the text of the New Testament stands absolutely and unapproachably alone among ancient prose writings."
F.J.A. Hort

A QUOTE TO CHEW OVER

"The interval between the date of the original composition and the earliest extant evidence becomes so small as to be negligible, and the last foundation for any doubt that the Scriptures have come to us substantially as they were written has now been removed. Both the authenticity and the general integrity of the books of the New Testament may be regarded as finally established."
Kathleen Kenyon, biblical archaeologist

"The Synoptic problem cannot be solved, can it?"

WHAT'S THE PROBLEM?
"How can you say that there is any integrity in the writings of Matthew, Mark, and Luke? They used each others' material when it suited them."

Synoptic
The word synoptic is made up of two parts:
Syn, meaning "together with."
Optic, meaning "seeing."
So the word synoptic means "seeing together"

Credit is due to J.J. Griesbach
The Gospels of Matthew, Mark and Luke are sometimes called the "synoptic" Gospels. In 1774 J.J. Griesbach first used this word "synoptic" to refer to the first three Gospels.

A careful reading of the four Gospels quickly reveals that Matthew, Mark and Luke are similar to each other and are in stark contrast with John's Gospel.

Matthew, Mark and Luke have:
• a similar viewpoint
• similar material
• a similar order of the events and sayings of Jesus

LOOK AT THE STATISTICS

1 Matthew's Gospel contains over 90% of the verses found in Mark's Gospel. Out of Mark's 661 verses 606 come in Matthew.

2 Luke's Gospel contains over 50% of the verses found in Mark's Gospel.
The substance of 350 out of Mark's 661 verses are found in Luke's Gospel.

3 Only 31 verses of Mark's Gospel have no parallel in Matthew's or Luke's Gospels.

4 Matthew and Luke each have about 250 verses not parallelled in Mark.

5 About 300 verses in Matthew's Gospel and about 250 verses in Luke's Gospel have no parallel in any of the other Gospels.

The Synoptic Problem

"Where did the authors of the synoptic Gospels get their material from?"

"Were the authors dependent on each other as they wrote their Gospels?"

"Did the authors go to a common source for their material?"

These kinds of questions concerning the original make up of each of the first three Gospels have given rise to what is called the Synoptic Problem.

Divine inspiration is not affected

No matter how the Synoptic Gospels may have been originally written by Matthew, Mark and Luke – Christians have always believed:

• that the Holy Spirit guided the thinking and writing of the Gospels writers.

• that the Gospels are part of Scripture and that "all Scripture is God-breathed." *2 Timothy 3.16*

WHAT'S THE CONCLUSION?

There is no loss of integrity since there was no conspiracy or cover up.

"Doesn't a prior source undermine the originality of Matthew's, Mark's and Luke's Gospels?"

WHAT'S THE PROBLEM?
"If Matthew, Mark and Luke used a source often called "Q", all you are left with is a scissors and paste job – not an original Gospel."

Q stands for *Quelle*
The verses in Matthew's Gospel and in Luke's Gospel which are common to each other, but do not appear in Mark's Gospel are often called "Q" material.

Quelle (Q) is the German word for "source."

The theory is that Q, along with Mark's Gospel, was used by Matthew and Luke as they compiled their Gospels.

THEORIES GALORE
The idea about Q is not the only theory alive today. Other suggestions about the origin of the Gospels include:

The priority of Matthew
This view says that Mark and Luke drew on Matthew's Gospel as they wrote. This theory assumes that Matthew's Gospel was written before Mark's and Luke's.

The existence of oral tradition
This view states that all the gospel writers used a well-known account of the life of Jesus that had been passed on by word of mouth.

The lost Gospel
This view suggests that the Gospel writers had access to another Gospel, which no longer exists.

Written fragments
This idea believes that short records about Jesus' actions and words were made during his life, and that the Gospel writers had access to them and used them.

A combination of various theories
Some scholars think that the Gospel writers made use of oral tradition, written fragments, each other's writings, as well as eye-witnesses to whom they spoke.

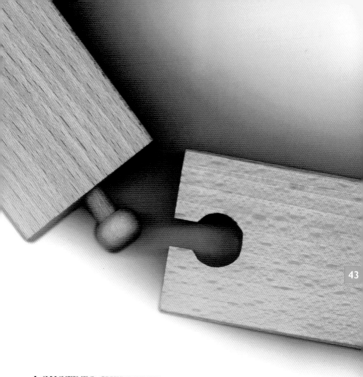

A QUOTE TO CHEW OVER
Source Criticism

"We must not fall into the error of thinking that when we have come to a conclusion about the sources of a literary work we have learned all that needs to be known about it. Source Criticism is merely a preliminary piece of spade-work.

"Who would think that we have said all that is to be said about one of Shakespeare's historical plays when we have discovered what its sources were?

"So also, whatever their sources were, the Gospels are there before our eyes, each an individual literary work with its own characteristic viewpoint, which has in large measure controlled the choice and presentation of the subject matter. In attempting to discover how they were composed, we must beware of regarding them as scissors-and-paste compilations."
F.F. Bruce, The New Testament Documents, IVP, 1992, p.44.

"Is there anything in the New Testament that can help us in personal suffering?"

WHAT'S THE PROBLEM?
"Does the New Testament offer any satisfying solutions to the problem of suffering when that suffering hits home at a personal level? Forget all the philosophical arguments. Does the founder of Christianity offer any help in the here and now?"

1. Jesus did not say that all suffering stems from our own particular sin

The Jews of Jesus' day were sure that if you suffered it was your own fault – it was on account of your own sin.

When Jesus "saw a man blind from birth, his disciples asked him, 'Rabbi, who sinned, this man or his parents, that he was born blind?'

"'Neither this man nor his parents sinned,' said Jesus, 'but this happened so that the work of God might be displayed in his life.'"
John 9:1-3

2. Jesus fought against mental and physical illness

When face to face with a person who was suffering, Jesus never adopted the attitude of passive equanimity.

When Jesus was confronted by disease he was affronted.

When he met the woman with the twisted body, he didn't sigh, or let her pass by. This was an affront to God's wishes for it was a malignant attack from Satan.

Jesus saw her, called her, spoke to her, put his hands on her and healed her.

The synagogue ruler was "indignant because Jesus had healed on the Sabbath."

Jesus exploded:

"Should not this woman, a daughter of Abraham, whom Satan kept bound for eighteen long years, be set free on the Sabbath day from what bound her?" *See Luke 13:10-17*

3. Jesus' healing work went beyond the physical

Jesus healed the whole person. He had great compassion on the physically ill, but he was also moved to the depths at the sight of people who needed spiritual help.

> "When he (Jesus) saw the crowds, he had compassion on them, because they were harassed and helpless, like sheep without a shepherd."
> *Matthew 9:36*

When the four friends of a paralytic brought him to Jesus everyone expected Jesus to say to him: "Get up, take your mat and walk." But Jesus first said: "Son, your sins are forgiven." *Mark 2:5*

The Master Doctor saw the underlying spiritual condition of the man, not just his physical ailment.

4. Jesus himself suffered

Matthew records how Jesus healed such people as: a man suffering from leprosy, the centurion's servant, Peter's mother-in-law and the demon-possessed. He then recalls some words of Isaiah, noting how they were fulfilled by Jesus.

> "He took up our infirmities and carried our diseases."
> *Matthew 8:17*

Jesus was literally the suffering Servant who took on himself all our burdens. When he died on the cross he shouldered our load of sin and shame and sorrow.

45

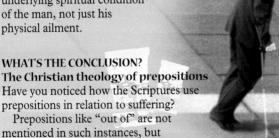

WHAT'S THE CONCLUSION?
The Christian theology of prepositions

Have you noticed how the Scriptures use prepositions in relation to suffering?

Prepositions like "out of" are not mentioned in such instances, but prepositions like "in" or "through" are.

> "Most gladly, therefore, will I ... glory in my infirmities, that the power of Christ may rest upon me." *2 Corinthians 12:9 KJV*

> "When you pass through the waters I will be with you."
> *Isaiah 43:2*

"In a scientific age can we continue to believe in the Virgin Birth?"

WHAT'S THE PROBLEM?
"Jesus could not have been born by a virgin: it is a contradiction in terms. On top of this, many ministers no longer believe such fanciful ideas."

Critics say:
Bishop David Jenkins once said, "I would not put it past God to arrange a Virgin Birth if he wanted to, but I very much doubt if he did."

Oxford theologian Keith Ward has written, "God could have become incarnate without being born of a virgin … So it is possible to believe that Jesus is the Son of God without accepting the Virgin Birth."

Most church leaders accept the Virgin Birth
The "Virgin Birth" should, more accurately, be called "the Virgin Conception".

The Anglican House of Bishops in England said in *The Nature of Christian Belief*:

1. "As regards the Virginal Conception of Our Lord, we acknowledge and uphold belief in it as expressing the faith of the Church of England."

2. "All of us accept that the belief that Our Lord was conceived in the womb of Mary by the creative power of God the Holy Spirit without the intervention of a human father can be held with full intellectual integrity."

Is a virgin conception possible?
Parthenogenesis, the technical name for virgin birth, occurs naturally in greenfly and bees.

Unfertilized rabbit eggs have been submitted to chemical and physical shocks and embryos are the result. It has been claimed that parthenogenetic rabbits exist.

What about the Y-chromosome?

For a human to be born like this the baby would need the one thing the mother does not have – a Y-chromosome. However,

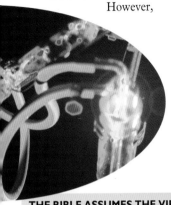

Professor R.J. Berry, of London University's Genetics Department, (a convinced Christian) states that an ovum in a woman with a particular type of chromosomal mutation develops without fertilization. The result would be a boy.

Professor Berry does not claim that this had to be the way Mary conceived, or that, even if geneticists could never come up with a way of making parthenogenesis possible in humans, that would not shake his belief in the Virgin Birth.

THE BIBLE ASSUMES THE VIRGIN BIRTH – IT NEVER SETS OUT TO PROVE IT

1. Gabriel's statement: "You will be with child and give birth to a son." *Luke 1:31*
2. Mary's response: "How will this be, since I am a virgin?" *Luke 1:34*
3. Gabriel's answer: "The Holy Spirit will come upon you, and the power of the Most High will overshadow you." *Luke 1:35*
4. Matthew's comment: "All this took place to fulfil what the Lord had said through the prophet (*Isaiah 7:14*): 'The virgin will be with child.'" *Matthew 1:22-23*

A DNA test

If a DNA test were taken on Jesus and Joseph would it indicate that Joseph was Jesus' father?

No. The biblical story indicates clearly that Joseph's DNA would not show up on a test.

A QUOTE TO CHEW OVER

"The biological mechanisms exist … it would be improper in the light of our knowledge of genetics and embryology to say virgin births can never happen." *Professor R.J. Berry*

"Did Jesus really die on the cross?"

WHAT'S THE PROBLEM?
Put quite simply: If Jesus never died on the cross there is no need for Easter Day and his resurrection.

Why is this such an important question?
Christians claim that the death and resurrection of Christ is the central plank of their faith.

Jesus made a startling claim about the resurrection. He said: "I am the resurrection and the life" *John 11:25*

It was the center piece of the first Christian sermons: *Acts 2:23-24.*

"The apostles continued to testify to the resurrection of the Lord Jesus." *Acts 4:33*

Without the resurrection of Jesus, Christians are a group of people with no hope. The apostle Paul said as much: "If only for this life we have hope in Christ, we are to be pitied more than all men." *1 Corinthians 15:19*

Without the death of Christ, there is no forgiveness and no salvation: *1 Peter 2:24.*

JESUS REALLY DIED

But, could he not have swooned on the cross and revived in the cool of the tomb? No!

1. Jesus had been flogged

He had been flogged probably with 39 lashes. Bones and lead attached to leather thongs ripped into the flesh of the person being flogged. No wonder Rufus had to be pressured into carrying Jesus' cross. Jesus was exhausted after enduring such a flogging.

2. Jesus had been crucified

The crucifixion was not performed without eyewitnesses. Jesus was crucified in public before a crowd of people.

3. Before he would release his body Pilate checked that Jesus really was dead

Pilate was surprised that Jesus had died so quickly. So he specifically asked a centurion to verify this. "Pilate was surprised to hear that he (Jesus) was already dead. Summoning the centurion, he asked him if Jesus had already died. When he learned from the centurion that it was so, he gave the body to Joseph (of Arimathea)."
Mark 15:44-45

Roman soldiers were experienced in recognizing death. Had this centurion been mistaken about Jesus' death he would have lost his own head.

4. Jesus had his side pierced

"One of the soldiers pierced Jesus' side with a spear." John 19:34
The spear must have entered Jesus' heart. For what onlookers took to be "a sudden flow of blood and water" (John 19:34) was blood and the fluid from inside the pericardium (the sac which surrounds the heart). This fluid looks like water.

5. The stone was rolled away

A big stone had been rolled in front of the tomb, Matthew 27:60, and Roman soldiers were left on guard, Matthew 27:62-65. Even if Jesus had recovered from a swoon, he could never have got out of the tomb.

49

WHAT'S THE CONCLUSION?

An open-minded study of the evidence leads to the conclusion that Jesus was dead when his body was wrapped and laid in the tomb.

A QUOTE TO CHEW OVER

"That cross is a tree set on fire with invisible flame, which illumines all the world. That flame is love."
Thomas Traherne, Centuries of Meditations

"Can dead people be raised?"

WHAT'S THE PROBLEM?
"We're just not in the habit of believing that dead people rise from the grave! Anyway, what evidence is there for the amazing claim that Jesus rose from the dead?"

So is there any evidence?
Here are three facts a skeptic must answer. A fourth one comes on the next two pages.

FACT 1

Jesus' tomb was found to be empty.

"Very early in the morning, the women took the spices they had prepared and went to the tomb. They found the stone rolled away from the tomb, but when they entered, they did not find the body of the Lord Jesus."
Luke 24:1-3

"BUT, couldn't these emotional women have looked in the wrong tomb?"
As Jesus was placed in a brand new tomb, *Luke 23:53*, it would be easy to identify.

FACT 2

Somehow or other, the body of Jesus was no longer in the tomb.

"The angel said to the women, 'Do not be afraid, for I know that you are looking for Jesus, who was crucified. He is not here; he has risen, just as he said. Come and see the place where he lay." *Matthew 28:5-6*

"BUT, couldn't the disciples have stolen the body and pretended that he had risen?"

After Jesus' resurrection these dispirited disciples became fearless preachers. Though it cost them imprisonment and flogging, they taught that Jesus had been raised from the dead.

Do men who base their lives on a lie manage to "turn the world upside down" *Acts 17:6 KJV*?

Would the first Christian martyrs have submitted to agonizingly painful deaths if they had known in their hearts that what they were saying was a lie or a nonsensical exaggeration?

FACT 3
The soldiers were bribed to say that the disciples had stolen the body. *Matthew 28:11-15*

"BUT, couldn't the leading Jews have stolen the body of Jesus?"

They might have been able to strike a deal with Pilate. But when they became totally fed up with the constant preaching about "Jesus and the resurrection" Acts 17:18, all they had to do was to produce the rotting corpse of Jesus. They didn't produce his body because they couldn't.

WHAT'S THE CONCLUSION?

It is not unreasonable to believe in the resurrection of Jesus. There's plenty of evidence to support it.

A QUOTE TO CHEW OVER

"No resurrection. No Christianity."
Michael Ramsey, former Archbishop of Canterbury

"Does the New Testament explicitly state how Jesus rose from the dead?"

WHAT'S THE PROBLEM?
"Why are so many church leaders tentative about or embarrassed about the reality of Jesus' resurrection? What is the person in the street meant to believe when even some top theologians have doubts?"

WHAT THE NEW TESTAMENT TEACHES

Jesus' tomb was empty

"But when they looked up, they saw that the stone, which was very large, had been rolled away. As they entered the tomb, they saw a young man dressed in a white robe sitting on the right side, and they were alarmed. 'Don't be alarmed,' he said, 'You are looking for Jesus the Nazarene, who was crucified. … He is not here. See the place where they laid him."
Mark 16:4-6

FACT 4
The body of Jesus was raised to life
"Why do you look for the living among the dead? He is not here; he has risen!" *Luke 24:5-6*

What would a video replay have shown you?
If you had a camcorder focused on the tomb where Jesus was buried on the Friday evening what would it have recorded by early Sunday morning?

Just how did Jesus rise from the dead?

The New Testament does not explain what a camcorder would have seen. It does not say exactly how Jesus rose again. It was achieved by the power of God: "By his power God raised the Lord" (*1 Corinthians 6:14*) ... but we are not told what method God used to achieve this.

The risen Jesus appears and disappears. Jesus could walk or appear through closed doors.

But the exact nature of the Jesus' resurrected body is never explained.

It's a mystery

Christians should not claim that they can learn and know everything about God from the Bible. The Bible only claims to tell us what God in his wisdom knows we need to know for our salvation.

There are many things we might like to know which the Bible is silent about. We may want to know more about what heaven will be like. We may want to know more about how Jesus rose from the dead. We may want to know the answer to innocent suffering. Yet, some things remain a mystery.

A QUOTE TO CHEW OVER

"A religion without mystery must be a religion without God."
Jeremy Taylor

"Were the appearances of Jesus after his death just hallucinations?"

WHAT'S THE PROBLEM?
"All the resurrection appearances of Jesus can be put down to wish fulfillment. His disciples and the women followers were so distraught that they would have believed anything. All they saw was a string of hallucinations."

The hallucination theory
There is one big flaw in the hallucination theory. Hallucinations don't happen to people who are not expecting them. The one thing Jesus' disciples did not expect, even though Jesus had taught them about this, was that Jesus would come alive again after his crucifixion.

An historical fact
No event in history is as thoroughly documented as the resurrection of Jesus.

> "I know of no one fact in the history of mankind which is proved by better and fuller evidence of every sort, to the understanding of the fair inquirer, than the great sign which God has given us that Christ died and rose again from the dead."
> *Dr Thomas Arnold, Professor of Modern History, Oxford University*

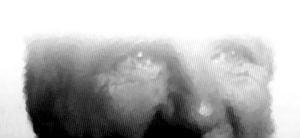

SO WHO DID THE RISEN LORD JESUS APPEAR TO?

Person/people	For what particular reason	Bible reference
Mary Magdalene	Jesus was Consoler	John 20:14-18
The disciples	Jesus restored their joy	John 20:19-20
Peter	As his Friend who would never forsake him	Luke 24:34
Two on the Emmaus road	As their sympathetic Instructor	Luke 24:13-32
Ten disciples	Giving them his peace	John 20:21-23
Thomas (with disciples)	Confirming his faith	John 20:26-29
Seven fishing disciples	As the Concerned One	John 21:1-23
To over 500 disciples	As the resurrection and the life	1 Corinthians 15:6
James	Assuring one individual	1 Corinthians 15:7
Eleven disciples	Giving them power	Acts 1:4-9
Paul	To convert him	Acts 9:1-19
Stephen	To welcome him into heaven	Acts 7:55
John on Patmos island	As Head of the church	Revelation 1:10-18

55

WHAT'S THE CONCLUSION?
Maybe these resurrection appearances can't be explained away for one very good reason – they happened!

A QUOTE TO CHEW OVER
"Most men live and die; Christ died and lived." *John Stott*

"Where does it say in the Bible that you have to go to church?"

WHAT'S THE PROBLEM?
"Look how terrible today's churches are!
Some people say ...

CHURCHES ARE
DIVIDED

CHURCHES ARE
UNFRIENDLY

CHURCHES ARE FULL
OF HYPOCRITES

So why should we bother with them?"

CHURCH BUILDINGS
1. In the New Testament the word "church" never refers to buildings, such as cathedrals or chapels.
In the New Testament Christians did not "go to church", but met to worship in other people's homes. Paul wrote, "Greet also the church that meets at their house." *Romans 16:5*
2. In the New Testament the word "church" refers to Christians.
So, when Saul "persecuted the church of God" (*1 Corinthians 15:9*), he was attacking Christians.

The Church is Jesus' body on earth
The New Testament writers use a number of metaphors to describe the church. A favorite one with Paul was of the church as a body, as Jesus' body on earth.
"You are the body of Christ," (*1 Corinthians 12:27*). Paul wrote to the undisciplined, divided and ignorant group of Christians who lived at Corinth.

WE NEED EACH OTHER

1. A unit
"The body is a unit, though it is made up of many parts."
1 Corinthians 12:12

2. Many parts
"Now the body is not made up of one part but of many."

3. The foot
"If the foot should say, 'Because I am not a hand, I do not belong to the body,' it would not for that reason cease to be part of the body."

4. The ear
"And if the ear should say, 'Because I am not an eye, I do not belong to the body,' it would not for that reason cease to be part of the body. If the whole body were an eye, where would the sense of hearing be? If the whole body were an ear, where would the sense of smell be?

5. One body
" … There are many parts, but one body." *1 Corinthians 12:14-20*

It's so easy to stop going to church

The first followers of Jesus were tempted, possibly out of fear, to give up meeting together for worship and fellowship. Why else would the writer to the Hebrews have issued this warning?

> "Let us not give up meeting together, as some are in the habit of doing, but let us encourage one another . . ." *Hebrews 10:25*

BY WAY OF ILLUSTRATION
Teresa of Avila pictured Christians as Jesus' hands, feet and eyes to do his work on earth:
Christ has no body now on earth but ours
No hands but ours, no feet but ours;
Ours are the eyes through which Christ's compassion is to look out on the world
Ours are the feet with which he is to go about doing good
And ours the hands with which he is to bless people now.

A QUOTE TO CHEW OVER

> "There is no way of belonging to Jesus Christ except by belonging gladly and irrevocably to the glorious ragbag of saints and fat-heads who make up the One, Holy and Catholic (Universal) Church!" *Bishop Geoffrey Paul*

"Does the Bible teach that everyone should be converted?"

WHAT'S THE PROBLEM?
"All this talk about "conversion" and being "born-again" smacks of emotionalism and of thousands of people being manipulated by a clever orator at an evangelistic mass meeting."

WHAT ARE THE ELEMENTS OF TRUE CONVERSION?
Conversion demands the turning-around of one's whole self – one's mind, feelings and will. Conversion is a change from going one's own way to going God's way.

The feelings must be involved, but not the feelings alone.

LOOK AT PAUL'S CONVERSION
Paul's conversion, dramatic though it was, illustrates the essentials of a true turning to God. It is recorded three times by Dr Luke.

Paul's conversion touched his conscience.
• He knew that he was kicking against the goads. *Acts 26:14*

Paul's conversion touched his understanding.
• He realized that the Jesus he was persecuting was the risen Lord. *Acts 22:8*

Paul's conversion touched his will.
• He obeyed Jesus. *Acts 22:10*

Paul's conversion changed his feelings.
• It now had new desires and longings. "For to me, to live is Christ and to die is gain." *Philippians 1:21*

See *Acts 9:1-19; 22:4-16; 26:9-18*

Born again
True conversion is not something one can accomplish by oneself. God's Spirit working in the life of an individual brings about the change, or as Jesus' words state: "You must be born again." *John 3:7*

As a result of this "new birth" someone becomes a child of God. *See John 1:12*

BY WAY OF ILLUSTRATION

• A cabbage may be an excellent cabbage, but it cannot be an animal without a new kind of life.
• A dog may be a wonderfully loving dog but it cannot be a human being without a new kind of life.

• A human being may be very good but cannot be a child of God without a new kind of life: God's Spirit.

WHAT'S THE CONCLUSION?

Whatever the outward circumstances, conversion is a conscious decision that must be taken by every man, woman or child in the privacy of their hearts. It is a new relationship with God.

A QUOTE TO CHEW OVER

Conversion involves a decision: deciding for Christ
Joshua challenged the people of Israel: "Choose for yourselves this day whom you will serve ... As for me and my household, we will serve the Lord." *Joshua 24:15*

"Since the Bible never mentions the word 'Trinity', why do Christians believe in it?"

WHAT'S THE PROBLEM?
"Believing in the Trinity is a bit like believing in three gods. But I thought that the Christian God was one God and not divided?"

Thank you, Athanasius
The Athanasian Creed, dating back to the 6th century, summarizes the Trinity in this way:

> "The Father is God,
> the Son is God
> the Holy Spirit is God,
> and yet there are not three Gods, but one God."

BY WAY OF ILLUSTRATION

A spring
"Think of the Father as a spring of life begetting the Son like a river and the Holy Spirit is like a sea, for the spring and the river and the sea are all one nature."

A root
"Think of the Father as a root, of the Son as a branch, and of the Spirit as a fruit, for the substance in these three is one."

A sun
"The Father is a sun with the Son as rays and the Holy Spirit its heat."

John of Damascus

TRINITY IN THE NEW TESTAMENT

Many verses in the Bible, while not actually using the word "Trinity", point in that direction.

"May the grace of the *Lord Jesus Christ*, and the love of *God*, and the fellowship of the *Holy Spirit* be with you all." *2 Corinthians 13:14*

The Trinity and the gifts of the Spirit

"There are different kinds of gifts, but the same *Spirit*.
There are different kinds of service, but the same *Lord*.
There are different kinds of working, but the same *God* works all of them in all men."
1 Corinthians 12:4-6

The Trinity and mission

"Therefore go and make disciples of all nations, baptizing them in the name of the *Father* and of the *Son* and of the *Holy Spirit*."
Matthew 28:19

The Trinity and our salvation

"*God* chose you to be saved through the sanctifying work of the *Spirit* … that you might share in the glory of our *Lord Jesus Christ.*"
2 Thessalonians 2:13-14

WHAT'S THE CONCLUSION?

"Let us not be misled by the foolish argument that because the *term* 'Trinity' does not occur in the scriptures, the *doctrine* of the Trinity is therefore unscriptural."
F.F. Bruce

A QUOTE TO CHEW OVER

"Every divine action begins from the Father, proceeds through the Son and is completed in the Holy Spirit." *Basil the Great*

"Is the 'unforgivable sin' unforgivable?"

WHAT'S THE PROBLEM?
"Do you really believe that there is a sin that is unforgivable? Do you really hold to that?"

What the unforgivable sin is not

Most people have no idea what the unforgivable is. There are many people who think that they are so "bad" that what they have done must be the unforgivable sin. The following is a list of some of the things people have thought the unforgivable sin to be.

• Murder
• Adultery
• Masturbation
• Blasphemy
• Having an abortion
• Not going to church
• A divorce

All these ideas are very wide of the mark.

Did Jesus ever say that there was any sin that would not be forgiven?

"Every sin and blasphemy will be forgiven men, but the blasphemy against the Holy Spirit will not be forgiven."
Matthew 12:31

What the unforgivable sin is

Jesus had just healed "a demon-possessed man who was blind and mute."
Matthew 12:22

The Pharisees said that Jesus had expelled demons by the power of the prince of demons, Beelzebub. So their unforgivable sin is attributing Jesus' miracle, which was performed in the power of the Holy Spirit, to Satan. The unforgivable sin is to call Jesus and his divine power satanic.

People who do this would never go to Jesus for forgiveness, as they are saying he is of the devil. So their sins will never be forgiven by God.

UNBELIEVERS

Some have theorized that the one sin that is unforgivable is the sin of "unbelief." That is to say that "unbelief" is the one sin that the blood of Jesus could not cover. Every other sin in the world can be forgiven, but if one fails to place one's faith in Jesus Christ and decides to remain in "unbelief" – then that sin of unbelief is not forgivable. It is a direct rebuff of the work of the Holy Spirit on one's heart.

ARE YOU WORRIED?

Anyone who is genuinely concerned that he may have committed the unforgivable sin, has not done so. For such a person will ask God for his forgiveness. It is only the person who does not think that he or she ever needs God's forgiveness, who may have committed this sin.

NO ONE IS TURNED AWAY

Jesus said, "Whoever comes to me I will never drive away." *John 6:37*

A QUOTE TO CHEW OVER

"There is only one person God cannot forgive. The person who refuses to come to him for forgiveness." *Anonymous*

"How can the Bible help me?"

WHAT'S THE PROBLEM?
"Supposing God does reveal facts and principles in the Bible – but these axioms are very general and for all people. How can he speak to me personally?"

Come with a need
Do not compartmentalize your life. Expect the Bible words to apply to you.

Ask specific questions
How do these words or the principle outlined here challenge, encourage or direct me?

Be attentive and expectant
A Bible passage suddenly strikes you as being particularly relevant, significant, bright, helpful or challenging. This happens when God's Spirit is speaking to you and your heart.

Be patient
It is generally over time that our inner spiritual ear is fine-tuned. And note – not everything is significant all the time.

Follow a Bible reading plan
Then your reading of the Bible will cover all God's revelation and you will read the passages in context.

WHAT'S THE CONCLUSION?
The Bible is spiritual food

"How sweet are your words to my taste, sweeter than honey to my mouth."
Psalm 119:103

A QUOTE TO CHEW OVER

"Bible laid open, million of surprises."
George Herbert, The Temple